Cyberkids 1

MW00416563

The Knockout

PAUL COLLINS

Illustrated by Peter Foster

Triple3Play sundance

Published by
Sundance Publishing
P.O. Box 1326
234 Taylor Street
Littleton, MA 01460

Copyright © text Paul Collins 1999
Copyright © illustrations Peter Foster 1999

First published 1999 as Supa Dazzlers by
Addison Wesley Longman Australia Pty Limited
95 Coventry Street
South Melbourne 3205 Australia
Exclusive United States Distribution: Sundance Publishing

ISBN 0-7608-4795-9

Printed in Canada

Contents

Chapter 1

The Jade Dragon

Ming Siou Loong was better at virtual
fighting than anyone else around. She
worked her virtual construct fighter like the
master she was. In fact, Ming was so good
that everyone called her The Jade Dragon.
And when her fighter competed, Ming wore
yellow, satin, pajama gear with a jade-green
dragon on the back. She was quite a sight!

And fight? Let me tell you—Ming's virtual
fighter won every time. Muay thai kick
boxing? No sweat! Tae kwon do? Too easy!
Karate? Pah! No one even came close.
Ming's fighter was the best!

5

I wanted to beat Ming more than anything in the world. Don't ask me why—I just did, but no one could. She had the game sewn up. Anyway, to take a crack at her, I first had to beat Lee Brookes. And if I beat him, he'd beat me up, for real!

Lee took on all challengers every Friday night. Anyone with ten dollars could try, but no one stood a chance. No one but Ming Siou Loong, and she didn't bother. Ten lousy bucks wasn't worth the trouble.

Ming was just so *cool*.

I went to all the tournaments, mostly to see Ming Siou Loong. I studied her moves. She was pretty slick. She moved the controls of her virtual construct fighter flawlessly. Rumor was that Ming had fought over a thousand bouts and practiced every night before bed.

Ming always used state-of-the-art equipment. Her virtual fighter looked like a combination of Supergirl and a sleek panther. In fact, lots of us called Ming's fighter "the panther." She always wore a white bandanna with black Chinese designs and a black *gia,* belted with a sash. Her hands, feet, and face blazed fire-engine red when she was powering up. It was truly an awesome sight and drew gasps of disbelief from the audience when she first appeared in the ring.

Lee was really ticked off that Ming wouldn't fight him. His anger got the better of him one Saturday night, and he challenged The Jade Dragon in front of a full house.

The challenger always gets to choose the martial art. Lee Brookes had chosen muay thai, probably because there aren't many rules. Elbow strikes and spinning back-fists are allowed, for example.

The Dojo Virtual Gaming Center was *packed.*
Kids from everywhere came to see Ming whip
the pants off Lee Brookes . . . but Lee also
had his fans. They were mostly the meathead types with long, scraggly hair, sneering
looks on their faces, and loud mouths.

The ref came out by the ring, but Lee didn't
wait for him to start the fight. Instead, Lee's
fighter came blitzing out of the blue corner
and leaped forward with a solid jab-kick.
Ming's fighter fell on her butt. Before she
could get up, Lee's fighter kneed Ming's
fighter in the face.

Most of the audience screamed, "Foul!" But Lee didn't care. Rules and fair play didn't matter much to Lee.

The ref warned Lee, but the damage was already done. Ming was down two points for hitting the canvas, and Lee only got a warning.

My heart sank. Lee Brookes couldn't possibly beat Ming Siou Loong.

He just couldn't!

Out for the Count!

Ming flicked her head as though she'd been physically struck. Her ponytails swung about like war banners, and her face tightened. I swallowed hard.

From then on, they fought more evenly. Ming's fighter danced around the ring, and Lee's kick boxer blocked and made countermoves. At the end of the first round, Ming was still two points down.

The second round went much faster. Lee's fighter was powerful, and his hits scored higher marks, but the bigger your specs, the slower you are. Ming had to score almost twice as many hits to make up for some of Lee's powerful blows, but she managed.

And Ming pleased the judges. She *always* put in the required eight kicks per round, and her fight was *always* spectacular. She did a ton of high kicks, even though the scores for them were mostly low. She did spinning side-kicks and jumping front-kicks. Her favorite was a spinning leg-sweep that usually dumped her opponent on the canvas, but, unfortunately, it only scored minor points.

Ming also pleased the crowds. Her black-robed warrior knocked out Lee's muscleman seconds into the sixth round.

You didn't need to look at their specs on the LED board in the center of the stage to know that both the fighters had lost power. They were starting to fade. That's what happens when your fighter receives too many hits to vital areas or does too many fancy moves. Exhaustion in a virtual fighter causes loss of power, just like it does in a real fighter.

Lee's notorious neon-blue fighter was looking pale and in need of a power charge. He was a goner for sure!

Ming's fighter came out of the red corner, leaped high into the air, and shot out her left leg. Her foot struck Lee's fighter right in the head. I swear you could almost hear the sound of his neck snapping back.

Lee glanced up quickly at the spec charts. He'd lost a fast ten points, and his fighter was already shimmering like a fading ghost.

Ming's fighter landed on the canvas, ducked under Lee's retaliatory left punch, and then leg-swept him.

The gong sounded. Lee's fighter simply vanished. The score: Lee Brookes, eighty-two points; Ming Siou Loong, one hundred points.

Someone cheered Ming. Then others joined in, and within seconds everyone was cheering and hooting.

Lee and his thugs glared at us and barged out of the Dojo Center. I ducked when he looked my way. No need to take risks, right?

Ming graciously let the applause wash over her. After all, she was the queen.

And I wanted to be the king. But to beat Ming Siou Loong—The Jade Dragon—I needed a fighter at least as good as hers. Actually, better, because I didn't have her experience.

Chapter 3

Nova's Prototype

That night I went home and begged Dad for two hundred bucks for a new fighter.

"Two hundred dollars?" Dad said. "You want two hundred dollars?"

"Yeah," I said. It seemed like a reasonable request. Mom and Dad had given my sister, Nova, two hundred bucks for her Science Achievement Awards entry.

"Go away," Dad said. "I'm reading the paper."

"You gave Nova a couple of hundred," I complained. Why is it that parents never want to discuss things?

"I said, 'Go away'."

Dad normally means what he says the first time around—the second time, he means business.

"Mom, can I have two hundred dollars?"

"Don, we gave your sister money for a worthwhile cause. If she wins, she's going to donate the prize money to the local hospital fund."

"Go figure!"

"That's why Nova gets two hundred dollars and you don't, Don. You should learn to think of others sometimes."

But all I wanted to do was make a name for myself. I was thinking about my future. What was wrong with that?

I desperately needed that money. First prize at the Science Achievement Awards was a thousand bucks. Maybe I should get on Nova's good side, just in case she won. She wouldn't give *everything* to charity.

I tapped on her bedroom door. "Hey, Nova? You want me to do kitchen duty for you tonight?"

"What do you *want*, Don?"

I tried her door—it was unlocked for a change. I poked my head into her room.

That's when I first laid eyes on her science project.

"Wow!"

Nova got up angrily and herded me back toward the door. "I'm telling Mom you got a key made to my room!" she shouted.

"I did not!" I yelled back. I tried looking over her shoulder, but she blocked my view.

Then Dad came up behind me.

"Don, how many times do I have to tell you to leave your sister alone? Get downstairs and empty the dishwasher. *Now!*"

"But it's not my turn!" I said.

"Don got a key cut to my room!" Nova screeched.

Dad groaned. "Don't be silly, Nova," he said.

I must have blocked out everything after Nova's accusation. I'd never thought of getting a key cut to her room. But since she mentioned it, maybe I would.

I don't even remember emptying the dishwasher. That two-second glimpse of Nova's science project was all it took to put me in a dream state.

Nova had put together an amazing virtual gymnast. She was plain, boring, all white, but so what? She had been doing back-flips when I'd poked my head through Nova's bedroom door. She had leaped at least three feet into the air and performed some totally awesome splits.

Oh, wow! What I could do with Nova's gymnast! She looked frail, but with a bit of creative tampering, I knew I could turn her into a fighter.

I'd beat Lee Brookes hands down. I'd flatten Ming Siou Loong in front of everyone.

I'd be invincible. I'd be king!

Chapter 4

Breaking and Entering

Getting a key cut to Nova's room wasn't as hard as I'd imagined it would be. She usually had a steaming, hot bath late at night before bed.

Mom and Dad were normally fast asleep by ten o'clock.

I waited for five minutes after Nova had climbed into the tub. I prayed that the bathroom door handle wouldn't squeak, and it didn't.

The opening door fanned the steam around the room, but luckily Nova had her eyes closed. It took me five seconds to get her bedroom key from her pajamas and another six seconds to push both sides into some soft clay. Then I got out of there as fast as I could.

I think if my heart had pounded any harder, it would've leaped right out of my mouth!

I fell asleep that night thinking of clever ways
to defeat Lee Brookes at the next Dojo meet.

It cost me a week's allowance for Art
Meecham to get a key cut from my clay
impression. Art was known as the "artful
dodger." If you wanted something, he could
get it for you—at a cost.

Getting into Nova's room when she wasn't there was more difficult. But, before getting too excited, I needed to get a real look at Nova's virtual gymnast. And I needed to know if she'd finger-coded it so that only she could handle its movements. If she had, it would be useless to me.

I was really tempted to go into her room that night while she was having her bath, but my thumping heart wouldn't let me. If Mom or Dad caught me, I'd be in *big* trouble. If Nova caught me in there, I'd be dead meat!

So I had to wait for Friday night. Mom and Dad always did the shopping that night and insisted that Nova and I go with them. As a joke, Dad called it "the family's night out."

I came down with a terrible "flu" Friday afternoon. All I had to do was smell some flowers, and twenty or thirty whopping great sneezes came out one after another.

Then I cut an onion in the backyard shed,
and my eyes watered like a dam had burst.
Some really hot water on my face finished
the job.

I was a mess. Mom sent me straight off to bed. I could've done without the vapor rub and the flu capsules, but it was all worth it.

At seven o'clock, Mom's car pulled out of the driveway. I gave them a good five minutes, just in case they forgot something. Then I ran to Nova's bedroom.

Would the key work? Art had warned me that it might need a little grinding down, but I'd been too scared to try it with anyone in the house.

My hands were shaking so hard it took three tries just to get the key in the lock. It went halfway in . . . and then it stuck. I twisted it and wiggled it and then tried shoving it in further. Finally it moved. I turned the key. It turned stiffly, but it worked!

I can't tell you how nervous I was. Maybe a little guilty, too, but mostly nervous. Every time a car went past our house, I ran to the window.

But I knew I had at least an hour, so I finally relaxed a little.

Nova's virtual gymnast unit was on her desk. It was a flat, black box about the size of a video player. The twin controls were a little unusual—they were mittens with finger slots. I switched on the unit and gasped. It was awesome!

Nova's virtual gymnast looked so flexible I figured she could have turned inside out without sweating. She now wore silver leotards and had real short-cropped hair. It was a shame, though, that she wasn't wearing super-duper martial-arts gear.

I'd never seen anything like it. My little finger twitched by mistake and she did a back-flip. I moved my finger again, and she reversed the flip before I could even blink.

Time got away from me. The slamming of doors and sound of voices woke me from my trance. The front door opened, but I still didn't want to leave the gymnast.

"Don? We're home!" Mom's voice called out. That's when I finally snapped out of it.

I shut off the power and watched, mesmerized, as the shining, silver gymnast vanished. I rearranged the control console, leaving everything the way I'd found it.

I had just locked the door when someone came running up the stairs. Nova appeared just as I got to the bathroom.

"You don't look too good," she said, and headed straight for her room.

A thought jumped out at me—her prototype would still be warm! "Hey, Nova," I called.

She looked over her shoulder. "Yeah?"

"You know how to use a thermometer?" I grabbed it from the bathroom cabinet. "Can you tell me what the thermometer reads?"

She came over and stuck it in my mouth.
"It's really quite simple, Don," she said.

Those few minutes gave the prototype time
to cool down and saved my bacon.

Chapter 5

Plans in Motion

I didn't sleep too well that night. I only had a little over an hour with Nova's virtual gymnast, but I'd handled her like a pro. We were made for each other. She was better than any fighter I'd ever seen.

I went through everything, over and over again. I even reread the *Official Virtual Fighting Manual.* There was nothing in there about fighters having to wear official uniforms, and it even encouraged prototypes. And it talked about some pretty cool-sounding virtual fighter constructs from Japan and China.

Nova's Science Awards night was in two weeks. If I was to fight Lee Brookes, it had to be next Friday. That left me a week to sneak in as much practice with Nova's gymnast as I could. And to figure out how to "borrow" it and return it to her room safely, without her even knowing it had left the house.

That week whizzed by. I booked in my challenge at the Dojo on Monday. That way I would be up first, at exactly eight o'clock. My folks would get home after nine. It was going to be close, but the rewards would be worth it!

Then I called Art in his "office" at home.

"Hi, Art. It's me, Don."

"What do you need, Don?"

"I'm fighting Lee—my challenge."

"I don't handle death insurance, Don. I don't have that sort of capital."

I laughed. Art's a real joker. "I just need a bodyguard."

"You can't afford that sort of army, Don. You'd need at least a high school kid. Maybe with two guys backing him up, you know?"

"What about your brother, Art? I only need him for one hour, max."

Art had to think that one over. I could just imagine him estimating the job on his calculator. "He's not cheap, Don. It'll cost you twenty bucks up front. Another twenty if he gets so much as a scratch in a fight."

My head spun. This adventure was costing me an arm and a leg. I'd have to empty my bank account! "OK," I said doubtfully. "I'll need him ringside at exactly eight on Friday night."

"Done." Art hung up.

During the week I was able to get in about five practice sessions. On Friday, I got the "flu" again and spent most of the day running to Nova's bedroom, practicing maneuvers with the gymnast, then running back to bed when I heard movement downstairs.

I still had the "flu" when Friday night arrived. "We'd better take you to the doctor," Mom said. "We'll drop you off on our way to the supermarket."

It was 7:30, and Mom was totally freaking me out. "I'm not *that* sick, Mom." I smiled my biggest fake smile.

"Then you'd better come shopping with us. You missed out last week," Dad said.

"I'm not *that* well," I said slowly, "and not *that* sick. It's one of those in-between things," I added hopefully. "Maybe you could just get me some juice or something."

Help came from an unexpected quarter. "Leave him here," Nova said. "It'll save you a fortune in candy and junk food."

"Good point," Dad said. "The shopping bill was twenty dollars less last week."

It was bait, but I didn't bite. "I'll be better next week—I promise."

They left at 7:50.

Chapter 6

Fighting Lee Brookes

I had Nova's virtual unit under my arm and was out the front door before Mom's taillights disappeared down the street.

I got to the Dojo Center at 8:03. The judge was in the process of giving Lee Brookes a win by default when I yelled out, "I'm here! I'm here!"

Everyone turned around. The judge looked grimly at his watch.

I think I set up in record time.

Lee Brookes shook his head sadly. He'd seen my ancient virtual units in the past. I'd bought most of them at swap meets—they just weren't in his league.

He punched his action-mode key, and his stocky virtual fighter buzzed with neon-blue life.

I started up Nova's gymnast. The moment she appeared, the audience broke up with laughter.

It was embarrassing, I can tell you. The gymnast was dwarfed by Lee Brookes's fighter. She looked totally outclassed, and I knew if I lost, I'd never be able to show my face in public again after tonight.

Since I was the challenger, I'd chosen tae kwon do, because it's seventy percent leg

work and thirty percent fists. With any luck, my gymnast's long legs would keep Lee's fighter at a distance.

The ref blew his whistle and signaled for us to touch fists.

I didn't bother with the formalities. My gymnast lashed out with a double front-kick to the face, and Lee's fighter hit the deck within the first second of the fight.

The ref cautioned me—my first and only warning in that round. I dared a quick look at the scoreboard. *Five points!*

Then reality hit home, and I looked over at Lee Brookes. He'd gotten up from his unit, and his friends were restraining him. Yowie! Surely he wouldn't try to kill me in front of witnesses!

I looked back to center stage. Lee had left his fighter standing there like a stunned moose.

I quickly spun the gymnast around with her left leg high for a crescent-kick. Lee's fighter hit the deck again.

Kids were standing up in the Dojo Center— they were screaming, they were wild. No one had ever knocked down Lee Brookes's fighter twice in the first round.

His fighter got back up and threw a flurry of punches at my gymnast. But he simply struck thin air. As soon as his fighter hit mine, my gymnast would either leg-sweep him or give him three kicks to the face before he could fight back.

The first round was a romp: Lee Brookes, fifteen; Don Sousa, sixty-five.

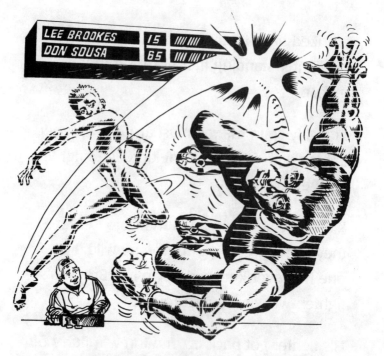

Just before the second round, I noticed Art's
brother, Duran, talking to a girl with long,
blonde hair. He was looking at his watch. She
was nodding, pleased by the attention. If I lost
my bodyguard, I was a goner.

I had to polish off Lee's fighter. I was taxing
the virtual gymnast to the max. I had her
jumping head high, kicking, landing, leg-

sweeping, and reverse-kicking. I even risked her doing some full-frontal punching techniques. I sincerely felt guilty about it, but I had to finish the fight as fast as possible—Duran was looking at the blonde and nodding toward the door.

A gong sounded.

Lee Brookes's fighter disappeared from the ring.

"Second-round knockout to Don *Sou-sa!*" the ref announced.

Lee Brookes and his meathead buddies tried pushing their way through the crowd. They were out for blood!

I was hardly aware of the cheering crowd, the thunderous applause, or the shrill whistles. Brooksy's murderous eyes followed me as I grabbed my unit.

I'd planned for this. I had my gear packed and was at Duran's side before anyone knew what had happened.

"I'll get you, you jerk! I'll kill you!" Brooksy yelled. But he couldn't get near me, because everyone was straining to get a look at me. *Me.* A hero.

Maybe they knew I didn't have long to live.

About the Author

Paul Collins

About the only distinguishing feature of Paul Collins's early teacher conferences was that teachers often accused him of daydreaming. He firmly says that everything he is writing now has been thirty-odd years in the making. He would like to meet those teachers again, if only to prove that he wasn't daydreaming at all; rather he was making up stories for when he left school.

About the Illustrator

Peter Foster

Peter Foster was born in 1931 and began to draw at a very early age. When he was just four years old, he got into trouble for drawing a canoe on the living room wall with his sister's lipstick.

In middle school he got into trouble for drawing comic-strip characters in the back of his math book. Finally, his dad found an unending supply of paper for him, and the years following were happily filled with drawing comics.

These days, he illustrates children's books and draws award-winning cartoon strips.